From M

Pouring out my heart in an attempt to make you see
I'm opening flood gates letting the waters run free
Touch doesn't have to be physical in order to be felt
Just a little warmth can make something frozen melt
I'll keep writing if there's a small chance of reaching you
I have other interests, but lately this is what I do
Since we're in this world together I think we should share
You're what's most important to me; that's why I care
I'll do my best to lift your spirits or at least I'll try
I want you to be optimistic, but cry if you must cry
Silence can be golden, allowing the words some rest
This is just insightful thinking, there won't be any test
I want you to enjoy your life in all that you do
Please accept this poem, as always, from me to you

A Fulfilling Life

Care giving because care is your thing
Entertaining others with the songs that you sing
Racing motorcycles, enjoying the fast lane
Seeking joy in a world of pain
Becoming a farmer and feeding the poor
The perfect gentleman, always opening the door
Conqueror of fears and helping others do the same
Coaching while advising much more than the game
Ministering to help others spiritually grow
Sharing experiences and all that you know
Fighting injustice and righting the wrong
Following your own road no matter how long
Loving unconditional, flaws and all
Helping the weaker when they need to stand tall
Climbing mountains to see the view
Closeness with God as you kneel at the pew
Cooking food as a culinary art
Volunteering because it's in your heart
Choosing to do what you love to do
Make life fulfilling and you'll be happy with you

A Good day

I slept in, because I could
I didn't pressure myself with the words "I should"
I thought good thoughts, and blocked out the bad
I told myself "I can't be happy if I'm feeling sad"
I stopped by the river and watched the water flow by
I became a little emotional, but I didn't cry
I walked the nature trail and enjoyed the view
I said hello to everyone, not just a few
I thought about love, or the lack of
I thought about God and the sky up above
I watched the sunset with a smile on my face
I found life more enjoyable at this much slower pace
I laid down to sleep and prayed my prayers
I realized I'm a good person and someone who cares

Alone

Being alone can be trying
You say its okay, but you might be lying
Sitting at the dinner table alone
The quiet house and the silent phone
You go to the movies just to distract
You'd love it if someone had your back
Opening the door as the key turns the lock
You step into the sound of that old ticking clock
People like your personality and say you're okay
You check the dating sites day after day
It's hard to share stories with no one to listen
Wanting a cooking partner while standing in the kitchen
Relationships sometimes can be hard to manage
It's quite difficult overcoming previous damage
Go live your life, and set free your past
Alone happens, but it doesn't have to last

Anxiety

Worrying about the bad that hasn't happened yet
The mind starts to race and it gets you upset
Your mind was focused, but now it's confused
You've convinced yourself you were born to lose
It's getting easier to become uptight
Tunnel vision has become part of your sight
The legs feel a little weak so you cling to a rail
You're not sure what to think and you look a bit pale
You don't want to be alone, yet people make you nervous
The doctor gives you a pill as part of his service
At first it was scary and hard to control
Now you're vigilant like a cop on patrol
Anxiety only makes more anxiety, that doesn't seem fair
You seek counseling from that intimidating black chair
Everything has a reason; at least you think so
Reading books on the subject because you have to know
Life is a challenge and the hurdles are high
You may never find the answers, but you still have to try

Appreciate

When I do a good job a simple wink will do
Please listen when I'm conversing with you
Stand by my side, not three steps ahead
Let me guide sometimes, instead of being led
I do the little things you take for granted
I run the bases so you can stay planted
Lifting you up all the time is no easy task
Recognize me, I shouldn't have to ask
Supporting actors usually have no name
They do the work while others enjoy the fame
If I could get half of what I give you
I'd be more content with the things I do
I'll give notice that it takes two
Appreciate me, like I appreciate you

Artist

A potter's clay takes shape with a gentle touch
A chef sprinkles ingredients, but not too much
Singers work feverishly on just the right tone
Sculptors see art in nearly every stone
A great actor can make you laugh or make you cry
Cinematographers are skilled at capturing the eye
Artists are people with tremendous vision
Add or remove is usually their hardest decision
The pen is a writer's friend when left all alone
Art on the walls make a house feel like a home
Engineers and carpenters see more than just plans
One uses a ruler, the other uses his hands
Photographers see things we take for granted
Images need a place, like seeds need to be planted
Bodybuilders strive to achieve that certain look
Authors spend countless hours writing a book
The world is a canvas and you have a color to add
We're all artists, and for that we should be glad

Attraction

A kiss is better when it's almost
Like brushing hands when we get to close
There seems to be no distance when we lock eyes
Our hearts tangled in knots; our legs weak in the thighs
It's flirting at its best without crossing the line
I can only imagine your warm body close to mine
It's evident just by the way we stare
We want to be together and breathe the same air
You carry yourself as if only for me
There may be a crowd, but it's only you I see
My mind has taking pictures that are mine to keep
I could fall in love with you, and fall in love deep
Body language speaks volumes if you have a good ear
We stand so far apart, but I can feel you so near

Back Of The Line

Given away as a child
Mother living in denial
Growing up way too fast
Early start to a messed up past
The teachers say I'm slow and falling behind
My hearts not in it; they seem so unkind
I don't like school, but I hate home
Most of the time I just want to be alone
It's a big world, but not for me
Seems like wherever I am, I'm not supposed to be
Turn off the emotions and get on with the day
Who am I kidding? I can't live that way
I think up alternatives to find resolve
Bad habits aren't bad if they help my cause
I know it's wrong, but what's so good about right?
Maybe someday I'll see the light
Like a flash of lightning it'll hit me fast
My mind will change and I'll be happy at last
No matter what happens, I'll be fine
Sometimes life's okay at the back of the line

Better Left Unsaid

I never wanted to know, but my heart certainly did
I tend to get lost easily, just like a kid
Like a movie where they leave out the last line
I prefer the answer now; you prefer later in time
The words withheld are locked up and you hold the key
Is it too much to ask if you could share them with me
You move freely and I feel bound
Silence speaks volumes and is very profound
If I didn't need the answer, you'd have no power over me
I could get on with my life; not as a prisoner, but free
Your voice is losing power and I don't care if you speak
You wanted to control me and make me weaker than weak
Some things can't be fixed and are better left unsaid
No need to answer the question; it's no longer in my head

Blues

My woman left me and went her own way
I can't stand my job or the lousy pay
My car is a relic and falling apart
My emotions are broken, just like my heart
I have high blood pressure and need to take pills
I perform blues music, but it never paid the bills
When I get home, the house is usually cold
I'm somewhat depressed or so I've been told
My guitar is in hock most of the time
I like good booze, but pay for cheap wine
The blues has consumed me, I know this for sure
However the notes heal me, just like a cure
When I listen to blues music it leads me to hope
It lifts me much higher then any kind of dope
It speaks to my heart and cleanses my soul
It's the one thing I can count on, especially when I'm low

Breathing

I watch you while you sleep
Your beautiful body under soft white sheets
Your face on the pillow and your cute button nose
The wind through the window gently blows
I want to kiss you and bring in the day
On second thought, I'll just watch you lay
The sunlight in the room shines on your hair
I won't make any noise, I'll just sit in this chair
I have things to do today, but this is a good start
Staring at you brings great joy to my heart
The stillness is just for a moment as you let out a sigh
I couldn't paint a better picture, so why should I try
You're the best part of me, the apple of my eye
I'll tell you I love you because it's so true
You're my happiness and without you I'm blue
Watching you breathing calms my soul
I love you forever and forever you'll know

Brothers

Black eyes and fat lips were a daily occurrence
We were both strong and we had the endurance
Our shiny black hair was longer then most
We were alter boys together, and we accepted the host
Our grades certainly never made our parents proud
We liked our music, and we liked it loud
We both liked the girls, and we certainly weren't shy
Growing up tough, meant you better never cry
The risks and mistakes are now unbelievable stories
All those injuries with very few glories
We settled down because our bodies finally said no
We're not getting any younger, and it's beginning to show
No more running and hiding, it's time to stay near
We're going to need each other to help conquer the fear
The road has been long, but we're still going to drive
Life is more important now; let's keep it alive
It's very rare I say I love you, but I most certainly do
You need me as your brother and I certainly need you

Can I Help You

You don't say much when it comes to your needs
Your garden is complete, containing only your seeds
Sure it's great to be self-reliant and endure whatever
You think it makes you sharp, knowledgeable, and clever
No one can help you; that would be collaboration
You have your own world, a self-sustaining nation
You refuse my jacket even when it's cold
You claim exercise will stop you from getting old
Doctors are okay, but you like holistic instead
You fall asleep naturally, never a pill by your bed
You prefer to limp instead of using crutches
You see things through, right down to the final touches
You'll get the door, as long as I walk through first
You carry around your own water just in case you thirst
You're afraid to ask for help because you don't trust
Sooner or later you'll find assistance is a must
Stop refusing help when it's offered at no cost
You'll find memories of help never get lost

Can't Fake It Anymore

You have a lover and I don't have you
Acting like I don't care isn't easy to do
We stay in touch because there's something we both need
Your lover might make you happy, but yet I intercede
You haven't pushed me away; in fact, we talk all the time
My emotions are scattered all over the ground
My love for you has now become more profound
Deeper are the feelings without even a touch
How can that be possible, loving someone so much
Is it just a dream I'm trying to keep alive
Other girls wink, but they can't catch my eye
My stare is reserved only for you
Perhaps I'm being misled and I don't have a clue
I know you like me, but I've come along too late
The story of my life sitting alone without any date
Someday a girl will want me and I won't see the sign
It might be my love for you that's keeping me so blind
My feelings are real and I can't ignore
I love you so much and I can't fake it anymore

Chances

Becoming vulnerable when getting close with others
Turning a friendship into something more like lovers
Thrill seeking when it means risking it all
Not recognizing a number and still answering the call
Paying for an education with no job in sight
Walking in the darkness when you can't find the light
Lending money that may never return
Willing to make mistakes in order to learn
Dating sites with only a picture to go by
Hoping on the truth when it feels more like a lie
Hearing the diagnosis and accepting the treatment
Taking a chance is a step towards great achievement
If you haven't kissed in awhile; it's high time you do
Drop the walls and barriers and give every ounce of you
There's setbacks with chances that later help you grow
If you don't take chances, how will you ever know

Children

The great joy a newborn can bring
Everything about them makes the heart sing
It's work, but a labor of love
They're a blessing sent from God above
Soon it's off to school and some trying times
The teen years are spent keeping them in line
Soon the empty nest becomes a lonesome place
Life has now slowed to a much quieter pace
They decided to marry and settle down
It's not often you see them around
You start to think you're last on their list
You recall when they loved to give you a kiss
They have jobs, but still hit you up for money
Some things never change and you find that funny
You still gladly give knowing they can't repay
You can't wait to be a proud grandparent someday
Where did the time go and how did it slip away
You realize you molded them, like a potter with clay
Such a responsibility, but you've seen it through
Hopeful when you get older, they'll return the favor to you

Confused

You say you love me, but won't hold my hand
You like music, but never see a band
You like going to dinner, but won't eat a thing
You want to get married, but won't wear a ring
You love flowers, but let them wilt away
You love sunshine, but stay inside all day
You like exercise, but you never workout
You get the right answer, but yet you doubt
You love reading, but don't open a book
You love fishing, but won't bait the hook
You like dancing, but never leave your seat
You want to be a drummer, but can't keep a beat
You like talking, but never answer your phone
You say you want company, but prefer to be alone
You like swimming, but dislike getting wet
You like gambling, but never place a bet
You sure are different, but I'm still glad we met

Content

As life goes on we deal with a lot
There's no pre-written story, not even a plot
Everyday unfolds by the minute
We should be happy just to be in it
We sometimes stand in silence and lament
However most of the time we prefer to vent
It's becoming hard to trust
Seems lately everyone's taking advantage of us
Time is moving faster then ever
Should have stayed in school, but wasn't that clever
There's pressure from all sides
No room to run or even hide
A second on a computer has become too long
Faster and faster till life's all gone
Everything has potential; we just have to look
It's not always hiding in some self-help book
We have to accept ourselves; perfection is never to be had
Let's not go there and end up sad
Life is like wine; it takes time to ferment
If we want it to taste good, we need to be content

Courage

I suppose courage is in me somewhere
When presented with difficulties or an occasional dare
It's not like wearing armor that everyone can see
Most days it remains hidden, even from me
I need to jump, but not sure how to land
I'll look to God, and ask for His hand
Courage isn't the absence of fear
It's more like pushing on when the danger is near
You don't need military training to be brave
You must address fear, wave after wave
It's not about showing off or "look at me"
It's about staying put when it's easy to flee
The mind says no, and the body wants to follow
Be courageous now and don't wait till tomorrow
When the ordeal is over, you'll feel much stronger
Fear becomes tranquil and restricts you no longer

Crossing The Line

When a line is crossed, you can't go back
The dream and fantasy have now become fact
Will the experience match the expectations
Will it leave us happy and filled with elation
Our minds always paint a picture of bliss
Can love ever be as good as the first kiss
Is that the top of the mountain, the highest we'll get
Saying it's only lust is something we won't admit
We may have been waiting for a long time
Everyone has someone, I want mine
Stepping over the line takes a lot of nerve
I think I've suffered enough and I want what I deserve
Being alone for a long time doesn't disqualify me
It just means love comes with no guarantee
What if we didn't call it a line
Rather a destination where your heart meets mine
I want us forever and I think its fine
Let's head in that direction and start crossing the line

Cry

What ails you my dear?
Speak up so I can hear
Your eyes tell me there's something wrong
It's not like you to be sad for so long
Is your heart broke and filled with distress?
Maybe you should give your thoughts a little rest
Clear your mind of all the wrong done to you
Fill your heart with joy; after all I still love you
Flowers, candy, a long car ride
Tell me what you need; I'll be right by your side
It's not about time washing the hurt away
Life is now, and it's a brand new day
I'm not saying not to feel
I just don't want the depression to become a big deal
The best thing about you is the smile in your eyes
Let's keep that going, even when you need to cry

Depression

The word no one wants to hear
Life's gotten you down it's certainly clear
The sky is gray even in sunlight
Getting out of bed takes up all your might
People say fix yourself up and put up a fight
Easy for them to say, living in the light
Time passes by as you wait on your saving grace
Difficulty is evident and it shows on your face
The days are longer when singing the blues
People tend to keep delivering nothing but bad news
Positive vibes elude and pass you by
Life seems bitter and it makes you cry
Is it your mind, or just the way you think
The answer isn't found at the bottom of your drink
Focus on the good, but deal with the bad
Life is far too important to be so sad

Diagnosis

Life of the party, but a solitary man
Willing to help others, but won't accept a hand
Outwardly open, but somewhat confined
Living in the now, but struggling with the behind
Embraces others, but finds it hard to touch
Longing for love, but not accepting too much
Playful as a third grader, but serious like the teacher
Believes in God, but not the best preacher
Likes going fishing, but doesn't want to catch a fish
Enjoys fancy restaurants, but orders the same old dish
Seeks change, but sticks to routine
Doesn't mind getting dirty, but is obsessed about clean
Reads books daily, but not sure what they all mean
Politically minded, but refuses to vote
Loves music, but is critical about each note
A walking contradiction, but isn't confused
He's like everyone else, this is certainly no news

Don't Be Afraid

Easy to say, but hard to do
It's no easy task becoming a braver you
Can the voice that says "no" be told what to do
You know your limits, only you can push you
What happens when no one holds your hand
How will you deal when life doesn't go as planned
Should you start a relationship or go it alone
We're all human and fearfully prone
You can't ride a bicycle if you're afraid to fall
What about darkness when you can't touch the wall
Confronting fear can be overwhelming, so take a small step
The only way to build muscle is rep after rep
So pick a weight, no matter how light
In time you'll handle more and build up your might

Don't Hold Your Breath

Your life isn't going as planned
You're not the type to ask for a hand
You take a drive to clear the mind
The best days seem distantly behind
The cigarette habit is getting expensive
You feel uneasy and a bit apprehensive
Your spouse doesn't understand how you feel
The little things have now become a big deal
Pacing the floor to digest the day's events
Your body's muscles are now rigid and tense
You heard meditation might ease the burden
Sounds foreign and you're not quite certain
This isn't the result you worked so hard to achieve
You feel trapped with no exit to leave
Giving up has never been your style
You hang your head as if on trial
Holding your breath will only affect you
Take care of yourself and do what you need to do

Dream

I had a dream I was holding onto
I did everything in my power to make it come true
This dream didn't require sleep to own
This dream covered me, like skin covers bone
This dream was for years, not just a night
This dream dissolved and is no longer in sight
It's painful that my reality has now become a fairytale
I can handle wind and rain, but this feels more like hail
I'll have to admit this is a great loss
When you dream big, sometimes you pay the cost
My daydreams will have to consider a new course
My dream was like a marriage, sadly ending in divorce
The romance of it all kept me anticipating
I'm afraid it's over, there's now no more waiting
Dreams are something the mind won't do without
I'll seek a new dream; after all, that's what life's all about

Embrace

How do you hold yourself when no one else will
Gazing at old pictures planted on the window sill
Leaning against the counter, coffee in hand
Listening to music from some old band
You're dealing with emotions that are hard to share
You'd like to be more open, but you just don't dare
Being alone should never indicate your worth
We're all individuals, starting right from birth
Appreciation is fine and we all need that human touch
Just don't go begging for it; that would be too much
It's up to you somehow to build your own strengths
Find happiness and take it to great lengths
Learn from solitude even in a crowd
Silence those voices that speak really loud
Tomorrow always brings in anew
Embrace who you are, what else can you do

Endure

The past is filled with scars that hurt the heart
It was a difficult journey in which you played a part
When an engine is blown, it's time to shut the hood
If you could fix the past, I'm sure that you would
You can't get far if you plan on standing still
Replaying the past will only make you feel ill
Stay clear of the rewind button, just stay on play
Give the past the once-over and then be on your way
Push forward even when you fall
You're not the first one; it happens to us all
You're in a race so you might as well run
Endure the clouds and you'll eventually see the sun

Excuses

Why is it so hard to accomplish my dreams
Too many distractions; or so it seems
Without excuses I'd be a busy bee
People would be expecting a great deal from me
If they can have excuses, than why can't I
In some ways, excuses are just a white lie
Excuses give me time to avoid confrontations
I'm glad, because I don't have nearly the patience
I'm starting to believe I really have other things to do
Now I'm treating myself like I treat you

Facial Features

The pink lipstick is a classic look
This face belongs in a fashion book
Firm cheekbones set "real" high
Hard to spot a wrinkle under those vibrant eyes
The right amount of freckles shown on her face
If she's wearing makeup, it would be hard to trace
Brunette hair with just a hint of highlight
Pearl white teeth making her smile just right
Her skin isn't pale, instead there's a natural glow
If she has imperfections, it certainly doesn't show
Her nose slightly pointed turned upward a bit
It's centered properly and it's a perfect fit
Her lips are unique and perhaps her best feature
Artistically speaking, she's an amazing creature

Faith

Believing in something I can't see
A chance to eradicate the doubt in me
Taking sometime to feel my soul
Faith may be the answer I'm longing to know
Life is bigger than my daily run
Scientists still baffled by the earth and the sun
I'll let faith flow through me like a gentle spring
Faith is God's gift without costing a thing
This faith is much more than just me
It's trusting in God, lock and key
Faith can't be replaced by any other emotion
It stands on its own when dedicating my devotion
When I'm scared and men's words no longer console
God's voice will fill me, in faith I know

Fashion

From heels to boots or no shoes at all
All the models on the runway so glamorous and tall
When on the red carpet you advertise your designer
Later reporters select who looked finer
From long hair to now bald with a beard
Fashion has even been considered bizarre and weird
The well-dressed have logos attached to their attire
Some kind of status symbol we're all suppose to admire
Fashion changes daily so don't spend too much
The look you have today, tomorrow will be out of touch
Chic, grunge, mod, vogue, hip or high
Fashion remains different to an individual's eye
Flannel shirts or tie and tails
Women walking around with decorative nails
I guess it's best that we don't all look the same
That would make life rather dull, boring and plain

Fear

All the things I wish I could be
Fears become an issue unkind to me
Risk is bigger than just one word
Quiet works better when afraid to be heard
I want to jump, but will my parachute fail
Fears attacking me like a storm with hail
It's wearing away one emotion at a time
It's got me balled up, unable to unwind
Is the water too deep or the mountain too high
I suppose it wouldn't hurt to give it a try
Growth comes when attempting the unknown
We can't go through life asking to be alone
It's not the first grade or a spelling bee
It's life with more and it's asking for me

Find Purpose

Gather strength, from all that you love
Embrace any chance to rise above
Be a sculptor or just finger-paint
Kiss so intensely, you could almost faint
Fly high and notice the curvature of the earth
Forgive yourself and start over like birth
Move forward and leave the past behind
Discover inner peace, then open your mind
Be the light and let it shine through
Hold hands, just your lover and you
Stop hiding and venture to seek
Keep pushing on, when you're tired and weak
Listen to music like it's performed only for you
Find serenity when you have a million things to do
Be a fighter and never drop your guard
Find purpose in life no matter how hard

Fitting In

Is it the look or the body type
Is it the popularity and all the hype
Is it the talent or the style of talk
Is it the fashion when out for a walk
Is it the education
Is it the status or need for elevation
Is it a belief system for one to subscribe
Is it keeping others out, expanding the divide
Is it the first class seat on every flight
Is it pushing a point just to be right
Is it driving the finest of cars
Is it hanging out in all the right bars
Is it the neighborhood with the high tax rate
Is it the best-looking person when selecting a date
Fitting in is exhausting and hard to maintain
Keeping up with the "In" crowd is a superficial game
Scrap the idea before you get in too deep
When you're you, it makes it much easier to sleep

Forgive Myself

You see me outwardly, but not from the inside
I carved out a little space in me where I often hide
Outwardly the smile seems so very bright
That smile doesn't linger when I'm alone at night
The road was rough and I'll take most of the blame
Destructive behavior seductively became part of the game
I can run all I want, but I can't lose the weight
I accuse myself constantly, as I had a hand in this fate
My colors get contaminated recounting my past
My body feels fully broken in need of a cast
Alcohol has never been cleaning fluid for the mind
The thoughts still weigh heavy, like a never-ending fine
God has forgiven me forever and a day
When will I understand the debt he sacrificially paid
From where I stand, I'll find my way to my knees
I want to learn forgiveness; teach me God please

Fresh Wounds

Is there an expiration date on feeling bad
The ups the downs and all the sad
The days and hours are suppose to heal
I wish the blues weren't part of the deal
I never thought a cut could be so deep
All the love dissolved unable to keep
I still believe in love, it's just going to take awhile
I know I'm hurt, but I refuse to live in denial
Taking part in this loss, I'll accept my share
Who would have thought a heart was so easy to tear
I'm strong even if a can't agree
The hard part is over and now I'm free
Someone will come along and attract my attention
I may be willing with a bit of apprehension
It will work out in the end; I can't view it any other way
Wounds heal, but it doesn't happen all in one day

From Where I Stand

I have my own view from where I stand
I'm attracted to you, but have no plan
I don't know your personality or your ways
Habits you might incorporate into your everyday
What kind of man would be suited for you
I'm sure I wouldn't get the nod or that I'd even do
The art gallery where one painting captivates the eye
You can tell the artist the truth and you don't have to lie
The colors blend and the texture is just right
The picture sticks in your mind both day and night
I'm simply an admirer because I enjoy the composition
I'll keep to myself, it's an easy decision
I'm not sure how long the painting will be on display
I'm just glad I had the opportunity to see it today

Further From Myself

As my hands reach out to hold onto the past
My life is slipping away all too fast
Nothing hangs on forever, it's not meant to last
Was I kidding myself all these years
Acting strong instead of confronting my fears
You made up this person because you didn't like you
There's millions like us, not just a few
People who just don't want to feel the pain
They become tired of the same old same
What if we had to examine our true core
Would we like ourselves less or slightly more
If not, there's always acting to get us by
It's getting old living out this lie
Fake it till you make it, or so they say
They don't have to walk around in our shoes each day
Sit down and become the real you
The faster you accept it, the better off you'll do

Good Things

The breeze flowing over your skin
A puppy dog's eyes when you touch his chin
A clean sweatshirt fresh from the dryer
A kiss from your lover's lips expressing desire
Helping an elder up from their chair
The smell of shampoo in your children's hair
The glow from embers when a fire subsides
Hanging at the amusement park enjoying the rides
Meeting new people and hearing their story
Memories of the old days, and all that glory
Being married for fifty years
Happiness so powerful it brings you to tears
Getting that great job you worked so hard to find
A strong body and a healthy mind
Friendships that will never end
Money in your pocket with extra to lend
Sitting by a river, lake or stream
Striving towards goals or achieving that dream
A long sandy beach with a beautiful sunset
Growing old peacefully without any regret

Happiness

Don't leave happiness waiting in the wings
Happiness can be found in the simplest of things
A walk on the beach with the sand between your toes
The smell of good cooking as it reaches your nose
A prayer to God right before getting out of bed
Planting positive thoughts as you fill up your head
Kindness and generosity without any reward
Finding silence refreshing instead of being bored
Making friends happy with just one smile
Walking a few blocks or running the whole mile
The peaceful sound of a distant train
No umbrella needed when dancing in the rain
A health report stating all is clear
Holding your grandma's hand as she draws you near
A clean house when you get home
That reassuring voice on the telephone
Happiness is a choice not an automatic thing
Whenever you get the chance, it's recommended you sing

Hard To Be Me

Falling in love can really sting
Just like a bird with a broken wing
Remembering flight and how good it felt
Now grounded with the cards that were dealt
When you push too hard, its easy to get burned
Some things must be experienced to really be learned
Taking a deep breath before going under
Drowning all the time is making me wonder
Should I smile more or dress in the latest fashion
I'm not selfish; in fact, I'm overflowing with compassion
I guess there's a checklist and I didn't pass the test
Left all alone like so many of the rest
Tomorrow I'll start anew
I'll start thinking less about me and figure out what to do
It's always hardest when pulling back on the reins
It's hard to be me when it comes down to pain
I'm not going to give up on this love endeavor
My heart will return--just maybe a bit more clever

Healing

So much suffering and pain over the years
The eyes dry after thousands of tears
We're all human and that's just part of the deal
We all have wounds that are difficult to heal
Age moves forward and takes what it will
Healing requires more than just one pill
You could walk in nature and find some healing there
It could be in a lover's eyes the deeper you stare
Traveling might work, but there's no place like home
Sometimes healing just means a little time alone
Faith can be miraculous, so keep that in mind
Sometimes it's okay to put yourself first in line
A nice back rub and a kiss on the cheek
A smile from a loved one when you're too tired to speak
Acceptance is hard, but from there you can endure
Always believe in yourself, that much is for sure
Healing can be found when you open your heart
Letting love in is the best place to start

Heaven

I believe heaven is the goal
The thing about it; it's up to your soul
You can't buy your way in or simply do right
The best we can do is follow God's Light
We'll see our loved ones and the truth will be revealed
All the wounds of this lifetime will suddenly be healed
Jesus said "I got this" as he lay on the cross
You may think you're in control, but you're not the boss
Heaven is a place with no expiration date
Turn to God now before it's too late
Beauty that last forever would certainly be admired
After a tough life, a place like that would be desired
The suffering will surrender as the soul finds a home
All of the lonely people will no longer be alone
Hatred and prejudice will no longer divide
We'll all love each other and be on each others side
You don't have to look up; He's standing where you are
God is omnipotent; He's much closer than far

Hope

Hope is important when our health is on the mend
It's a wonderful word when delivered by a friend
It's the expectation things will fall into place
It represents a good outcome in a difficult case
When we can't see the finish line, hope improves our sight
Hope brings the slightest of darkness into light
Embracing hope is like a gentle touch
Without hope, things don't mean quite as much
It's not an emotion; it's more like a need
If we want flowers, we must first plant the seed
Hope is not strength, but it can be just as strong
Hope embraces life, like a melody to a song
When things are broken, hope might speed the repair
Hope is like oxygen when we're starving for air
Never underestimate the importance of hope
Without it, we greatly reduce our chances to cope

I Can't Tell You

I'm afraid of my feelings for you
You'll probably say you never knew
Pining away like a little schoolboy
Like a child clinging to his very first toy
There's something between us, this much is true
I know my part, how about you
The hints I'm dropping aren't hard to see
I wish we could talk about it, just you and me
We could picnic in the park or under a tree
I could express my inner thought, and all that I see
Fear of rejection weighs heavy on my mind
Although I can't picture you as being unkind
I can't describe how your eyes pierce my soul
That information you may not want to know
I'd tell you, I want to be with you wherever you go
We could discover together the things we want too know
Sooner than later, you'll figure me out
My love for you has no shadow of doubt

I Love You So Much

Spent the day thinking of you
Your smile, your eyes, that pretty hairdo
All that shimmering black hair in the light
Those beautiful eyelashes batted just right
The smell of your body and the opium perfume
Your laughter infectious as it filled the room
Your voice feminine with just the right tone
When I was around you I never felt alone
The body of a woman with such style and flair
Everything about you made me stop and stare
Your heart was warm like a summer day
You gave me joy to feel the same way
It's not often one finds a gem like you
One in a million, far and few
I still recall the touch of your lips
You always gave such a wonderful kiss
The silly jokes and holding hands
How lucky I was to be your man
This poem wasn't written to make you blush
I wrote it simply because I love you so much

I Still

I still have dreams that push me along
I still listen deeply when I hear a great song
I still exercise even though it doesn't show
I still read books to learn more then I know
I still move forward even when I'm down
I still smile a lot when my friends are around
I still look to God to renew each day
I still speak up when I have something to say
I still write poems as a way to release
I still have anxiety, but praying for peace

I'm Getting Better

As a youngster, my life was a simple game
My days were all different, no two the same
Grade school was fun except on report card day
My favorite class was recess when I'd go out to play
Chicago field trips got me extra money for lunch
I had wild friends and we stayed a tight bunch
High school came and the girls caught my eye
I was very outgoing, but inside I was shy
Concert shirts and cut-off jeans; that was the fashion
Rock music spoke to me and I listened with passion
Motorcycles, dirt bikes, and a few fast cars
I have plenty of stories and I can show you the scars
I wasn't ready for children, but I'm glad I'm a dad
The marriage was challenging and the divorce pretty sad
The factories were for money, but not my cup of tea
It's a process, but I'm learning to accept me for me
My goals are in the present and that's where I'll be
I've had my troubles, but I'll work to make it right
Negative without positive is like darkness without light

I'm Sorry

I'm sorry for the things of my past
I'm sorry for all the love that didn't last
I'm sorry for the dark clouds on a sunny day
I'm sorry for not communicating what I had to say
I'm sorry for not affording you more attention
I'm sorry for my behavior and the unnecessary tension
I'm sorry for not really understanding
I'm sorry for being selfish and way too demanding
I'm sorry for all the things I neglected to do
I'm sorry for myself, because I don't have you

It's Okay

Sometimes we need to just give in
Fighting battles with no chance to win
Accidents happen; it's not always our fault
Good intentions don't always yield good results
Spilled milk is not a one-time occurrence
Life is long, we'll need the endurance
Heartaches happen, and it's hard to address
Friends console, but that doesn't fix the mess
Work is hard and the bills seem to get higher
We'll never really obtain all that we desire
We can't control every step of the way
Cards are dealt, and they lay where they lay
Trade perfection in for "job well done"
Having a little is better than having none

It's Time

It's time to love deeply with passion and concern
It's time to ask the teacher to help you learn
It's time to think before you talk
It's time for you and your loved one to take that walk
It's time to see the world with loving eyes
It's time to understand why someone else cries
It's time to read, write, or plant a seed
It's time to feed the hungry or help others in need
It's time to call and just say hi
It's time to tell the truth and put an end to the lie
It's time to appreciate your employment
It's time to embrace life with a great deal of enjoyment
It's time to talk to strangers and hear their story
It's time to praise God and recognize His glory
It's time to look at the leaves, not just the tree
It's time to release the past so your future is free
It's time to kiss and then kiss some more
It's time to be open, not a closed door
It's time to smile as bright as you can
It's time to be a loving husband, father, and man
It's time to be the mother, girlfriend, or bride
It's time to share the love you have stored up inside

Just Be You

There's a temptation just to fit in
No ones alike; not even a twin
You can't waste a lifetime thinking you're second best
Enjoy what you have, don't worry about the rest
Live and be alive; it's your world to explore
Run down every hallway and open every door
There might be a million people, but none like you
Narrate your life, and then make it come true
Don't tell yourself "others are better then me"
Negative self talk only makes you trapped not free
Life isn't measured by height, weight or size
If you seek the truth, you won't be affected by the lies
Don't just like yourself, use the word love
You hold purpose granted from God up above
Acting is fine, but is the show working for you
Don't worry about ticket sales, just do what you do
Facades are temporary, and crumble in time
Just be you, and things will always turn out fine

Just Blue

Crying takes up time, and I don't want you to see
Parts of my life are personal and only for me
The emotions well up when I think so deep
It can happen at night, and then I lose sleep
A sad movie is best to watch as the tears begin to flow
After all, I don't want anyone to actually know
Thinking positive and staying strong
That sounds easy, but it takes so long
It seems everyone is wearing a smile, all except me
I don't like my surroundings, wish I could flee
I'll do my best to make some repairs
My attitude should change as I clean up my affairs
I'll back off on listening to blues music all the time
I'll change the radio station in my mind
Perhaps a positive DJ with a supportive voice
I think right now that's my only choice

Last Line

Writing poems and thinking up rhymes
Assembling structure and words by design
It's difficult to build something that flows
Something different that no one else knows
A rough draft is the best place to start
You can't go wrong if you write from the heart
The deliverance is important and so is the pace
Poetry takes time, unlike a race
Should a line support or stand on its own
If you can't think of a line, it's best to leave it alone
Pick a subject matter that appeals to all
The worst is to deliver something boring and dull
Write a line when it pops in your head
Keep a pen and paper right next to your bed
I'm not sure there's really a last line
There's only more words gathering in the mind

Life's A Journey

When things are good, life seems to work fine
There's also the darkness at certain points in time
Life changes everyday when we step out of bed
The way we choose to view it, is how we'll be led
Mistakes never stop happening, no matter the age
Life is like a book, we can learn from each page
Setbacks are just part of the deal
Scrapes and bruises somehow eventually heal
The road isn't always one straight line
The work is hard, but we develop in time
We must learn to walk before we can run
Life's a journey, not every step is fun
Homework must be done before each test
The ones paying attention usually do the best
Happiness is perhaps the most important part
Love is essential, like blood to the heart
Life is more significant than just a few things
Dark winters tend to yield beautiful springs

Looking Back

Changing classes or works first bell
It's not just the images; it's the sounds as well
The vacation or that long summer day
The time your lover first looked your way
Learning to swing a hammer or turn a screw
Visiting the animals at the nearby zoo
Changing diapers while holding your nose
Siblings spraying each other with the garden hose
Your grandma's house with that slamming screen door
The dark times when you see loved ones no more
Oh to be able to change some of the rearview mirror
Unpleasant memories tend to stand a bit nearer
Thunderstorms threatened and so did the wind
Scrapes and bruises now stories on skin
Racing cars and empty beer cans
Digging the music and loving the bands
Crazy antics done on a whim
So much energy wasted trying to fit in
The first kiss, such a crowning moment
The sins to follow and seeking atonement
Looking back will never change a thing
Stay in this moment and sing if you can sing

Loss For Words

My tears don't need a voice; they can speak on their own
Suddenly I like seclusion and the thought of being alone
The weight is heavy and I feel every ounce
My broken heart is evident, why should I announce
If I opened my mouth the pain would flow out like a stream
The quiet days are memorable just like a recurring dream
I'll grin and bear it, as my lips stay sealed tight
I choose the darkness if words represent the light
The burden of love always shows up at the end
Once an excited lover, reduced to just another friend
I'll pretend not to notice you picked someone else over me
I'm not sure happiness is all about being free
I love you even if I can't say it out loud
My words now unrecognizable like a stranger in a crowd

Lost

You can't be lost if you don't know where to go
Where is your direction and why don't you know
Wandering aimless because the mind won't rest
You read the books, but didn't understand the test
At this stage in life you should have been found
You missed your turn while out driving around
People fly by and have places to be
What's so clear to them that you just can't see
You're a live wire that can't find a ground
The current keeps flowing without slowing down
You're not really a gypsy; the travels are in your head
It's your house, but it doesn't feel like your bed
The blood will still pump and the mind will still race
Never catching your tail, but never abandoning the chase
Lost isn't a bad thing, if the scenery offers a view
There are many maps, find the one that best fits you

Love

Love such a difficult word to say
Emotions and feelings getting in the way
I even dream about love in my waking hours
Will it shine on me, like sweet sun showers
I don't want to rush and be mismatched
I just want love, no strings attached
How many promises does one have to make
Giving love without acting fake
How many dates till one knows for sure
Love is best when it's simple and pure
Does one partner love more than the other
A good question that will soon be discovered
Flirting and smiling like there's no tomorrow
Love even hurts and can bring great sorrow
Love gives the heart wings to soar
Receive it, but always give back more and more

Love's Exit

Did we forget to hold hands or look into each others eyes
Did we hide the truth or just volunteer the lies
How did we let love just walk out the door
Love wasn't a pleasure; it was more like a chore
Did we forget to sweep when the house filled with dust
Leaving us short of breath and lacking in lust
Your eyes in the beginning gave off so such light
Now your eyes are dim and your lips sealed tight
It's been forever since we made love and felt those joys
We went from infectious laughter to barely a noise
I imagine when having a fire you must have a flame
Love's exit is unfortunate; let's not place the blame

Nature

The winds blow where they will
Man delivers a toxic spill
The birds land in the ocean
Man concocts radioactive potion
The grass grows green
Man litters majestic scene
Clear water streams
Fish filled with mercury, how unclean
Amber waves of grain
Dead crops from acid rain
Lakes deep and blue
Microbes and bacteria clinging to you
Water to quench our thirst
Bowls fill with dysentery; what could be worse
Farm fields to grow our food and make our meals
Toxic chemicals used for a larger yield
Beautiful sun
Ozone layer almost gone
Lofty mountains with white peaks
Nuclear plant springs a leak
Earth renews itself and strives
Man disappears and no longer occupies

Not All The Rest

In a gravel-filled driveway, you can still pick one stone
I want you to smile when my number rings your phone
I'd like to be your sunshine when all you see is gloom
We can be the happiest couple in a people-packed room
When troubles pile up, I'll help you haul them away
Tell me with your eyes and I'll understand what you say
If you want a hand to hold, mine is offered for free
I'd like you to feel loved whenever you're around me
When you're sick, I'll be the one who cares
I'll fight off the challengers and take on all the dares
I'll work extremely hard to ensure you have the best
My love will be waiting on you, not all the rest

Only Thoughts

We have thousands of thoughts each day
We cling to a few while others slip away
Believing them all is not what you want to do
Don't let the negative ones become a reflection on you
Positive is great and we sure hope it's real
Thoughts deliver emotions so it's a big deal
Deep thinking is commendable, that's well and fine
Seek quality not quantity when filling your mind
Gather good thoughts like saving coins in a cup
If your cup is half empty, optimism will fill it up
Thinking you're always right may be cause for concern
Knowing everything leaves very little room to learn
Don't be too hard on yourself and live in the now
If you don't know something, humbly ask how
You have a lifetime of thinking to do
Be kind to yourself and enjoy being you

Overreact

I've fallen in love with the notion
A kiss from your lips would set my heart in motion
It's as if I've been drinking a powerful love potion
You intoxicate me with every subtle move
My eyes fixed on you, like art work in the Louvre
Mona Lisa's smile has got nothing on you
You have better cheeks and a nicer hue
What should I say, and what should I do
All my attention is focused only on you
My senses become active when you come into view
What's a man to do when he's so in love with you
Pull it together, I tell myself
I don't feel this way with anyone else
My heart is yours and that's a fact
When you're around, I simply tend to overreact

Passion

Passion isn't reserved just for romance
When you feel it, chase after the chance
Follow your dreams even if they cost you at times
Don't follow all the rules, cross a few lines
Don't just listen to music, go buy a guitar
Travel and push your boundaries farther than far
Swim and stay wet on the beach
Attend church and listen to the preacher preach
Read as many books as it takes to feel smart
Paint pictures when the colors fall from your heart
Pick yourself up no matter how far the plummet
Climb your own mountains, making each step a summit
Help others whenever the opportunity appears
Awaken each day and try to conquer your fears
When a loved one needs you, stay close by their side
When the waves come crashing, ride out the ride
Tears are for a reason, it means you care
Accomplishments happen when you dare to dare
Passion makes you feel alive
It's like gripping the wheel the faster you drive
Grip passion for all its worth
It's one of the best feelings you'll find on this earth

Peace

We don't need negativity and stress
It only leads to a life of so much less
Wear a smile and shake a hand
Start being nice to your fellow man
Do the right thing and keep the peace
See your anger as a sign, not a release
Encourage others, but don't over-police
Lay down that weapon, the one you prefer to use
Whether it's your hand, fist or gun
The prison sentence won't that much fun
Peace is an ongoing process, one not to ignore
Violence tends to keep knocking; stay clear of that door
Our weapons have given us the final word
No one deserves that kind of power, to inflict such pain
Are we that bold or just that vain
Peace has to start, one person at a time
Deep in our hearts, yours and mine

People

What motivates them to meet each day
Do they like their jobs or is it just pay
Some have partners, while others are alone
Some fear loneliness as they stare at their phone
They appear to have a good life and I hope they do
I'm sure they have issues just like me and you
Will they make memories with each passing day
I'm sure some feel discarded or even in the way
People face seasons and the weather sometimes shows
There's no way to predict the future; no one really knows
The ones that worry seem to be stuck in time
There are others who look forward, never behind
Some love themselves and have good self-esteem
Others compare their looks to a glamour magazine
Most people have dreams, while some can't sleep
There are people hurting as their pain runs deep
People need people even when they say no
You can't just say I love you; you have to let it show

Positive Thoughts

The mind likes to point out the wrong
It's a habit that can last far too long
For every bad thought, find one good
It's like planting a flower in a bad neighborhood
Positive thoughts don't grow overnight
Negative is a contender and will give you a fight
You can't deny your struggles or hide your pain
The mind needs discipline like an athlete must train
Positive thoughts keep depression at bay
Refresh the mind like the springtime in May
Don't lie to yourself; if it's bad then it's bad
Remember sad moments help us appreciate the glad
Compassion, gentle and kind will represent the good
Soon flowers will blossom all over your neighborhood

Present Moment

Wouldn't it be easier to let the mind rest
Live in the now and give it your best
Look in the mirror and smile at yourself
You're you, no need to be somebody else
When you walk, look deep into the trees
Enjoy the wonderment of the flowers and the bees
Smell the air and feel the wind on your skin
Have fun in the game, don't anticipate the win
Pinch yourself and feel the sting
Tell yourself worries have never fixed a thing
Plan for the future, but accomplish in the now
You know what to do, stop wondering how
The past is gone and the lessons were learned
You can't go back, so don't be overly concerned
It's not easy stopping the thoughts in your head
Clear your mind daily before going to bed
Wake in the morning and rejoice in the new
Practice this often and become a happier you

Rainy Days

What's so wrong about rainy days
People seem only interested in bright sun rays
What's so bad about a little downtime
Rain is cleansing and helps clear the mind
Sitting in the car, watching the raindrops fall
Listening to music and thinking about it all
Time to be alone as the gray fills the sky
The birds are still singing as they gracefully fly
Rain is the best smell on earth
Moisture absorbed brings new life like birth
The trees become laden and almost look lazy
It's all natural and simply amazing
The rivers swell and swallow the land
Fisherman waiting with their poles in hand
Children jumping in puddles and getting muddy shoes
The paint on the car looks shiny and new
Sharing an umbrella brings us closer together
When there's small talk, it's usually about the weather
Rain on the roof and the stillness of night
If only for that moment, everything seems alright

Remain In Sight

You're amazing and I like what I see
I'd like to think you feel the same about me
Were you blinking or was that a wink
Was that a signal or just something I think
Our eyes have conversations that always make me smile
I envision us together mile after mile
The language of love is best spoken with the eyes
It's the eyes that project how hard the heart tries
I like staring contests because I have your attention
You're beautiful, my eyes will continue to mention
Your eyes shimmer, almost like a wet tear
My pupils dilate quickly whenever you're near
My eyes are usually active till you come into view
Once you're around, my gaze stays fixed only on you
When my eyelids are shut, you remain in sight
Day after day, night after night

Routine

Wake up and do it again
Same old day, same old end
No need to stress a mind on auto control
Going through the same day I already know
The menu might be different, but it all tastes the same
Has my life become empty or just terribly plain
The minutes I waste don't seem that many
When actually they add up to plenty
Life's not over and it's certainly not lost
When the door opens, light fills the room
It's a new beginning minus all the gloom
The first instinct is the old comfort zone
Stay clear of that idea and leave it alone
We must walk before we run
Lose the routine and go have some fun

Self-Aware

How you see yourself, is how you'll feel
You don't need to fake it; you just need to be real
Every day, hold your head up and be more aware
Do your best for others to show that you care
It's all external and you can choose what to let in
Wear a smile and lose that awkward grin
Don't abuse your body with this and that
You're not a guinea pig or a laboratory rat
Respect yourself and always seek knowledge
You don't have to be a professor or even attend college
Talk to an elder or open a book
Once in awhile, go to the mirror and have a good look
See beyond the image to what really counts the most
Treat yourself well and be the perfect host
Work hard to succeed, but don't forget to play
Wake up every morning and thank God for each day

Side Effects

It's not just related to a drink or pill
You'll find plenty nowadays to make you ill
The marriage that feels so depressing
The horrible job that keeps you stressing
The hard life on the wrong side of the track
When your best friend stabs you in the back
Children rebelling the more you keep them in line
All the laws and all the fines
Failing grades translating into poor-paying jobs
Court hearing resulting in anger mobs
Gambling excessive till you lose the farm
Still smoking after knowing the harm
Unprotected sex and the related disease
Loss of respect while doing what you please
Talking constantly just to be heard
Spouting profanity like an ordinary word
Thoughtfulness can reduce the side effects on you
Remember to think before you do what you do

Speaking Of Nature

Nature is speaking extremely loud
Man won't listen, he's way too proud
Let's burn some coal or start fracking some rocks
Black smoke from diesel trucks as they leave the docks
Cars could be more efficient, but who wants that
Rivers far too dirty, even for the rat
The polar ice is shrinking far too fast
Alaskan summers now warmer than the past
Glutton for resources, utility companies devour them all
EPA makes recommendations, but where's the law
Chemicals are dangerous, the doctor will say
Just put your boots and gloves on if you want your pay
Why clean up the mess, when we can just pay the fine
We can always haul the waste further down the line
The rain forest stripped of its treasure
What is it about destruction that brings such pleasure
Soon we'll be overheating as the AC roars
Now victims of the damage we created outdoors

Start Anew

I can't believe all the things I've done wrong
Sometimes life seems extremely long
My parents were hard on me, my kids claim the same
Put it all together and there's plenty to blame
The loveless marriage with the big wedding cake
Wearing a smile, but feeling like a fake
The old girlfriend whose heart I broke
Failed relationships ending on a bad note
Drinking too much and acting like a fool
Everyone does it; I'm no exception to the rule
That's not really true; I just want it to be
We all have things in our past we don't want to see
I can't fix everything, but I can always start anew
Give me that chance and I'll become a better man for you

Talking

We talk all the time, but haven't met just yet
I'm falling for you, that's a sure bet
I hear your voice in every word you send
My heart was damaged and you're helping it mend
I guess staying apart means playing it safe
My love would only multiply if I were to see your face
If you hugged me just to say hello
Tears would fall and I couldn't let go
I'd lose my voice as the words go still
I might even feel lovesick or a little ill
My heart leads me around nowadays
Navigating emotions somewhat like a maze
I'll use your love to guide me around each turn
Getting to know you is something I'm longing to learn

The Next Love Waiting

We probably should have never been
Love lost feels like such a sin
It's something that we can't undo
We live, we learn, and then we accept the view
We long for love and we take our share
We blame each other when it's not there
It's hard to accept the ending has come
It's time to look back on all that we've done
Why is love difficult; one really can't say
Heartache is depressing when it's getting its way
There's a bright side to this if we just step back in line
The next love waiting might last for all time

The One

There's always that one, no other will do
You might like them, but they care nothing for you
Your skin longs for their touch
Even a little love would be good enough
They like someone total opposite of you
You can't figure it out; I guess you're not supposed to
Try molding yourself to fit their needs
Even go as far as to cry and plead
Love letters, what a waste of good ink
All those silly words like water down a sink
The drug called love has confused the mind
However, the effects are pleasant; the most welcome kind
The One pulls your heart stings till the final note
Yet their love is clearly your best antidote

The Unknown

Will my foundation hold steady on shaky ground
Will my friends disappear or always be around
Will my plants grow after I planted the seed
Will love provide what I so desperately need
Will my children love me when I get old
Will I believe in things I've always been told
Will having money make me feel secure
Will my bravery slowly give way to my fear
Will my memory remain sharp as a tack
Will I suffer regret whenever looking back
Will my dreams become a thing of the past
Will there be a difference between first and last
Will I still have energy to see the job complete
Will I enjoy winning or be okay with defeat
Will I be content when I find myself alone
Will heartache become something I've outgrown
Will I forever waste time thinking about the unknown

There Comes a Time

At first I was strong and ready to fight
There's something satisfying about being right
My jaw was tough as I wore a stone face
I was the fast one, no other could keep pace
If they could lift heavy, I could lift more
The job was mine even before I hit the door
My head was up and my shoulders stayed back
I could run by myself, I never needed a pack
I could punch with the best and I could handle a blow
As time passed I learned a few things I didn't know
I don't like drama and it's been years since my last fight
I've been wrong as many times as I've been right
My eyes are now gentle and my face is less taxed
I'm never in a hurry and my body feels more relaxed
I still go to the gym, but I avoid the heavy weight
I'm lucky to have a job when I punch in at the gate
I feel good about myself; no need to stand tall
I love my friends and I'm happy when they call
I like to watch boxing, but I won't jump in the ring
There comes a time when it's a blessing not to be king

They're Not Interested In Me

My pockets aren't deep, in fact they have holes
Jeans and t-shirts are the extent of my clothes
My car is a four-cylinder not a fancy V8
I write impressive profiles, yet never have a date
If you robbed my house, not much will you find
I'm a thinker, but they're not interested in my mind
I'm genuine and never expect more than I can give
I can't deliver promises so I'll live how I live
Being up front and honest is the best way to go
They say what they want; I say it's good that they know
It's okay if they're not interested in me
I'll find the right one and then we can be "we"
My list of qualification consist of few demands
I'd like a warm heart, smile and gentle hands
No need to search the world, I'm only looking for one
When our days are cloudy, we'll be each others sun

Things I Tell Myself

It's no big deal; you should be able to cope
You're probably just afraid or giving up hope
If others had these problems, they'd know what to do
They'd seek out solutions, why can't you?
You should be strong and brave without fears
You should stop crying and wallowing in your tears
If you tried so hard, the results certainly don't show
You act so smart, but what is it you know
Having everything in order, but what is it you own
You claim to be social, but spend countless hours alone
Tons of great ideas that have yet to earn a penny
If you kept score, the mistakes would be many
You think worrying is the best way to care
That might be the reason you're losing your hair
Reading books, but forgetting the content
Always explaining to others exactly what you meant
These are only voices that aren't always true
Don't go around believing everything you tell you
They're all broken records and the songs are getting older
Its time to stand up and become increasingly bolder
Talk back once in awhile and turn down the sound
Remember you're a good person and a joy to be around

Things That Hurt Me

Don't roll your eyes, it makes me feel small
Don't push aside your emotions and put up a wall
Don't release my hand when others are around
Don't yell at me, I can't handle the sound
Don't look at me as if you barely care
Don't desire others with your occasionally stare
Don't give me the silent treatment as we lay down to sleep
Don't smile when I'm feeling the need to weep
Don't boss me around with your hands on your hips
Don't turn up your nose and frown with your lips
Don't act sweet just to get your way
Don't laugh when you see I'm having a bad day
Don't tell me there's always the door
Don't say you love me, then hurt me some more

This Time

This time I'll learn from my past
I'll use stronger line whenever I cast
The waters are deep the further I wade
I've seen the sunshine, now I'm longing for the shade
Things that were discarded still leave a mark
I can't move forward if I can't shift out of "park"
The images in the rear view mirror need to fade
This is my reality; I may never have it made
I need to live my life and not worry about what I possess
It's not about more, sometimes it's about less
This time I won't get caught up or be told what to do
I'll accept my plate, but I'll choose what to chew
Regret tends to come from wasting time
I'll find a clean glass, before drinking the wine
Artists don't become artists overnight
There's plenty of wrong; I'll look for the right
These are just words on this given day
This time I'll check the price tag, before I have to pay

Time Is Continual

The wasted years don't recycle, and they never will
If you made a mess, it's time to clean up the spill
History is formed one second at a time
Scribbling is fun; just remember there's a line
If you're feeling stressed, try writing a journal
Take time to purge and keep troubles external
The past is visible in a pair of aging eyes
Compiled experiences might translate into wise
Dreaming is fine if you do something with the dream
Make sure the boat floats before sending it downstream
There are loving moments that leave a timeless impression
The rough times are unavoidable and go without mention
Time is continual, so make the most of each day
Count your blessings even when life isn't going your way

Time

The hour glass reminds us with each grain of sand
Life's complicated and rarely goes as planned
It's said that time goes by in the blink of an eye
Make every minute count, or at least really try
Young people have fun and the clock is no concern
Later time is the teacher and that's how we learn
We think time will deliver love if we patiently wait
Love is in the now; don't wait till it's too late
The hours bring darkness that give way to the light
Some days we sing the blues and others we're alright
Don't watch the clock; the pace has always been the same
Its better to be free, don't make time a ball and chain
Dreams take action if you want them to mature
Remember time is a gift, not something too endure

Undressing love

Clothes cover the body as to not reveal
Words have two meanings, so what's the deal
In love one day and not the next
Wanting a phone call, not just a text
From talking all day to just hello
Guess I did something wrong, but I don't really know
Adding more layers instead of stripping them down
It's become very clear you don't want me around
I felt undressing love would relieve some inhibition
I should have spent more time examining my position
I don't want to go though life covered in regret
It didn't end well, but I'm still glad we met
Picking up clothes, one garment at a time
Adding all these layers is almost a crime
Love should be naked, beautiful by design
The more layers I put on, the less I feel
Clothes like bandages might help me heal
Once again I'll stand naked and be true to myself
That should make it easier when loving someone else

What Matters Most

Little things account for a lot
A cold drink of water when it's hot
Clean clothes on your back each day
The roof over your head and the bed where you lay
Shoes that fit your feet
Food in the cupboard with plenty to eat
A hug from a grandparent or a kiss on the head
When someone loves you no words have to be said
Friends through thick and thin
The smile on your kid's face when their team wins
Holding hands on a long walk
A phone call for no reason, just simply to talk
Autumn when colors dress the trees
The bandage from your mom when you skin your knees
The teacher who wants you to be smart
When you find it safe to give away your heart
Money in the bank when the mortgage is due
The moment you start accepting you for you
Art in any form or fashion
A single kiss filled with loving passion
The chance to follow your dreams
Life's not a rehearsal, it's an ongoing scene

Wild Side

It's their nature, people say
They choose to go through life acting that way
Always defiant and ready to fight
Being different brings them delight
Maybe it's the music that drives them wild
Maybe it's the way they were raised as a child
As soon as they settle, they're ready to leave
They say it's about freedom and space to breathe
Taking orders is not really their scene
They don't split hairs or get caught in-between
Risk is how they like to roll
Sometimes at the cost of a heavy toll
Blazing a trail we don't understand
They walk with danger, hand in hand
Independent personalities gambling all the way
They seemingly live life day to day
Thrill seekers by default in search of elusive glory
Being conservative is not part of their story
We admire them, but don't follow that route
We like structure to minimize our doubt

Wondering

What are the odds of me winning lots of money
Would I be happier if everyday was sunny
Would taking big risk pay off in the end
Does being generous make me more friends
What's love feel like and how will I know
When can I forget the past and let it all go
If I work through my problems, do I get a second chance
Will I ever be good enough for true romance
Does working forever make me a success
If my attitude was different, would I still be a mess
If I didn't control everything, would things turn out fine
I wonder when I'll stop wondering all the time

Young But Once

Most of us are broken and looking for repair
If the pain gets unbearable, it's time that you share
If you want love, you have to give love too
Move beyond the old and be open to the new
Try to do as many things possible with each passing day
If you don't like drama, better watch what you say
If you want a connection, step closer to the touch
The things that matter, rarely cost that much
Depression is an acquaintance, not a permanent date
Start calling on happiness, it's never too late
You can't be content when you have the urge to control
If it's peace you desire start nurturing your soul
You're young but once, never wait till you're old
Enjoy the brass ring now if you can't afford the gold

The Coming Winter

The droplets of rain dance on the ground
The wind wisps as it carries its sound
The birds hurry to build their nests
The forest creatures settle down for a long rest
The windows close and hold back the cold
The green leaves now give way to the gold
The trees strip themselves of their wilted attire
The backyard parties now include the warmth of a fire
The days shorten and the grass no longer grows
The weather is unpredictable; only Mother Nature knows
The fruit trees surrender up their final yield
The farmer's tractor leaves behind a barren field
The lack of sun gives the world a serious look
The blankets come out, and its time for a book
The first snowfall will soon be near
The silence of the season is wonderful to hear

I've

I've seen more then my fair share
I've felt like drowning, even with air
I've cried and couldn't shake the pain
I've given love and given love in vain
I've sang the blues and I could write you a song
I've tired to patch it up, just to get along
I've smoked and drank with the very best
I've struggled when it came down to the test
I've gambled right down to my very last dime
I've broke the rules and I've paid the fine
I've talked to God and I've been redeemed
I've had a rough life or so it seemed
I've worked hard to turn it around
I've been lost and I've been found
I've thought about a great many things
I've heard about freedom, but can't find the wings
I've found acceptances can free up the mind
I've found that if I seek, then maybe I'll find
I've wondered when my ship would come in
I've lost at love, but I still hope to win

Made in the USA
Charleston, SC
21 July 2016